CALENDAR

OF THE

NEW YORK CITY CHARTER

GIVING ALL TIMES FIXED BY THE CHARTER AT OR WITHIN WHICH THE MUNICIPAL OFFICERS ARE TO PERFORM CERTAIN DUTIES, ETC., ETC.

WITH INDEX.

PUBLISHED BY THE CITY CLUB OF NEW YORK
19 West 34th Street, New York City,
JULY, 1900.

1837
ARTES
SCIENTIA
VERITAS
LIBRARY OF THE
UNIVERSITY OF MICHIGAN
TUEBOR
SI QUAERIS PENINSULAM AMOENAM
CIRCUMSPICE

CALENDAR

OF THE

NEW YORK CITY CHARTER

GIVING ALL TIMES FIXED BY THE CHARTER AT OR WITHIN WHICH THE MUNICIPAL OFFICERS ARE TO PERFORM CERTAIN DUTIES, ETC., ETC.

WITH INDEX.

PUBLISHED BY THE CITY CLUB OF NEW YORK
19 West 34th Street, New York City,
JULY, 1900.

NOTE.

This calendar was designed to be a feature of a little book planned by the Municipal Government Committee of The City Club as a compact presentation of the framework and the operation of the government of New York City. Although much of the preliminary work has been done, it does not seem desirable to publish the projected volume until the revision of the charter now in progress has passed its final stage. But this fragment is now published in the belief that it will be of some service in connection with the work of the charter revision commission.

It is believed that such a statement of prescribed times and seasons as is here presented will be found to be of material assistance in an effort to determine the relations subsisting among the various departments and officers of the city government. This is indicated by the relatively large index to the calendar. Thus, for instance, the entries under "Reports" in the index cover about two pages, each entry marking a prescribed time for the making of a certain official report.

An effort has been made to state in simple language the substance of the provisions cited. In some cases the language of the charter is quoted at length because its meaning is somewhat uncertain, or because it presents peculiarities which make it difficult to paraphrase.

The many provisions of the charter for the monthly payment of salaries of this and that officer are not included. In the absence of any general provisions upon this point, it is sufficient to say that the general policy of the charter is that salaries shall be paid monthly.

One consideration has contributed largely to the decision to print this calendar upon the eve of changes which may be expected to affect some of the law stated in the following pages. The duties to be performed by the municipal officers at certain times are here stated so plainly that it becomes easy to inquire as to whether and how these duties have been performed. The fact that the charter contains these provisions will be news to many who will see this calendar. The City Club would be glad if citizens, taking this information as a basis, would pursue the inquiry suggested. Have these duties been performed? If not, why not?

CALENDAR OF NEW YORK CITY CHARTER.

[*References are to the Charter as in force after the session of the legislature of 1900. The fact that a section has been amended is noted only in case the amendment affects the subject of the entry in the calendar. In every case in which a provision relates to more than one day or period, it is repeated under each appropriate heading*].

IN JANUARY.

The **commissioners of accounts report** to the **mayor** and the **municipal assembly** "the amount of money received into the treasury" during the year ending the last day of the preceding November, the amount paid out, and other particulars as to the city's finances. —*Charter, section* 195.

The **police commissioners** as trustees of the **police pension fund, report** in detail to the **municipal assembly** "the condition of the police pension fund and the items of receipts and disbursements on account of the same."—*Charter, section* 351.

Until the 17th of January, 1907, the treasurers of the nine funds which share in the "tax upon the receipts of foreign **fire insurance companies** doing business in the borough of Brooklyn" render to the **fire commissioner** "a sworn statement as to the expenditures of said funds."—*Charter, section* 809.

The **Comptroller reports** "in detail to the **board of education**" "the condition of" the **public school teacher's retirement fund**.—*Charter, section* 1,083.

The members of the **board of health** as trustees of the **health department pension fund, report** in detail to the **mayor** "the condition of said fund and the items of their receipts and disbursements on account of the same."—*Charter, section* 1,331.

In every sixth year, beginning with 1898, the **mayor** appoints ten **marshals of the City of New York** —*Charter, section* 1425.

"There shall be published in the **City Record** within the month
" of January and within the month of July in each year a **list of all**
" **the officials and employees** employed in any of the departments,
" bureaus or offices of the city government, and of the counties
" therein contained, who have been or have become such officials or

" employees during the preceding six months. Said lists shall contain " the name, residence by street numbers, nature of position or service, " date of entrance into the service or employment, date of cessation of " such service or employment, if such has occurred during said period, " salary or wages, and a distinct statement of the increase or decrease " thereof during said period of each of said officials or employees."—*Charter, section* 1,528, *as amended by chapter* 615, *laws of* 1900.

FIRST MONDAY IN JANUARY.

At noon the term of office of " each **member of the council** " elected at the last preceding election begins, in every fourth year, beginning with 1898.—*Charter, section* 20.

At noon the first meeting of the **council** in each year is held.—*Charter, section* 22.

In every even numbered year the term of the **aldermen** elected at the last preceding general election begins.—*Charter, section* 24.

At noon on this day in every even numbered year, the **board of aldermen** holds its first meeting, and chooses one of its members to be **president of the board of aldermen.**—*Charter, section* 26.

At noon on this day in every sixth year beginning with 1898, the **council** elects a **city clerk** for a term of six years.—*Charter, section* 28.

On this day in every third year beginning with 1898 a **board of pharmacy,** composed of " five competent pharmacists" is selected in the manner provided —*Charter, section* 1,513.

SECOND MONDAY IN JANUARY.

From this day until the 1st of May, the books entitled " The Annual Record of the Assessed **Valuation** of Real and Personal Estate of the Borough of ———," are kept open " for examination and correction," " in the several offices established by the **department of taxes and assessments.**"—*Charter, section* 892.

Between this day and the 1st of May, the **deputy tax commissioners** designated for the purpose in each borough " receive applications for the revision and cancellation of any assessments entered in the books of annual record of the **assessed valuation of** real and personal estate" in that borough, "take testimony on such applications," and make recommendations to the department as to the applications—*Charter, section* 898.

On or before this day, the **deputy tax commissioners**, or "such other persons as may havc been assigned to take charge and direction of any one of the offices of the department of taxes and assessments in the several boroughs," compute from the annual record of **assessed valuation** "the total aggregate amount of the assessed valuation of real and personal property" in the borough, and "transmit a statement of such aggregate amounts of assessed valuations" to the main office of the **department of taxes and assessments.**—*Charter, section* 899

THIRD WEDNESDAY IN JANUARY.

The **mayor** appoints three members of the **school board for the Borough of Queens**, and three members of the **school board for the Borough of Richmond,** to serve for three years.—*Charter, section* 1,061.

JANUARY 1st.

At noon, in every fourth year, beginning with 1898, the term of office of the following **officers**, elected in the precedings November, begin:—

The **mayor.**—*Charter, section* 94.

The **comptroller.**—*Charter, section* 97.

The **president of the council.**—*Charter, section* 18.

A **president of each borough.**—*Charter, section* 382.

Four **coroners** in the Borough of Manhattan, two in the Borough of the Bronx, two in the Borough of Brooklyn, three in the Borough of Queens, and two in the Borough of Richmond.—*Charter, section* 1,570.

The terms of all **heads of departments, commissioners,** and other **officers** appointed by the mayor, "shall, as to those first appointed, commence at noon on the first day of January, 1898, and

" thereafter at noon on the first day of January, in the year in which " the terms of office of their predecessors expire, except that any person " who shall be appointed in pursuance of this section to fill a **vacancy** " shall hold his office for the unexpired term of his predecessor".—*Charter, section* 118.

" No vessel other than **canal boats,** barges or lighters, receiving " or delivering property from or to said canal boats or barges, shall use " or enter into for the purpose of using any part of the port of New " York, set apart for the use of canal boats and barges, without the " written consent of the **board of docks** had and obtained therefor, " and then only between the first day of January and the 20th day of " March in each year, and when not occupied by canal boats."—*Charter, section* 866.

Upon **taxes** for the previous year unpaid at this date, interest at seven per cent. a year calculated from the date of the delivery of the assessment rolls and warrants to the receiver of taxes, is charged.—*Charter, section* 916.

It is the duty of the **receiver of taxes** " to charge, collect and re-" ceive upon all **taxes** remaining unpaid on and after the first day of " January interest at the rate of seven per cent. per annum, to be calcu-" lated from the day on which the said assessment rolls and warrants " shall have been delivered to the receiver".—*Charter, section* 917.

Between this day and the 15th of January the **board of education** files "a record of its apportionment of the **general school fund,"** among the boroughs, "with the **Comptroller**".—*Charter, section* 1,065, *as amended by chap.* 751, *laws of* 1900.

On or before this day **each board of inspectors of common schools** makes its quarterly written **report** to the proper **school board** " in respect to the condition of the schools, the efficiency of teachers " and wants of the district, especially in regard to schools and school " premises".—*Charter, section* 1,098.

" No person shall kill or expose for sale, or have in his possession " after the same has been killed, any robin, meadow lark or starling

" between the first day of January and the fifteenth day of October".—Certain cases are excepted.—*Charter, section* 1,493.

JANUARY 10TH.

On or before this day, the **municipal civil service commissioners** make a **report** to the **state civil service commission.**—*Charter, section* 125.

[NOTE.—The general civil service law, enacted as chapter 370 of the laws of 1899, does not repeal specifically the parts of the charter relating to the municipal civil service commissioners. These parts of the charter are, however, superseded by the law of 1899, so far as they are inconsistent with it. Under that law every municipal civil service commission makes an annual report to the state commission on or before the 15th of January.]

JANUARY 15TH.

The **receiver of taxes** may issue to any **city marshal** a warrant for the collection of any unpaid **tax** for the previous year with interest at seven per cent. a year from the date of the delivery of the assessment rolls and warrants to the receiver.—*Charter, section* 926.

The **receiver of taxes** may recover, with interest and costs, the amount of any **tax** on personal property levied for the previous year and remaining unpaid at this date.—*Charter, section* 936.

Between the 1st of January and this day the **board of education** files " a record of its apportionment of the **general school fund,"** among the boroughs, "with the **comptroller.**"—*Chapter, section* 1,065, *as amended by chap.* 751, *laws of* 1900.

SECOND WEDNESDAY IN FEBRUARY.

The **school board** in each borough elects one of its members **president of the board,** and also elects " its delegates, if any, to the **board of education.**"—*Charter, section* 1,089.

THIRD MONDAY IN FEBRUARY.

The **board of education** elects one of its members **president of the board of education.**—*Charter, section* 1,062.

FEBRUARY 1ST.

The **mayor,** the **comptroller,** and the **chamberlain,** by a majority vote, fix the rate of **interest** to be paid by banks and trust companies upon the city's daily balances during the ensuing three months.—*Charter, section* 196.

. Every agent of a **foreign fire insurance company** in the city pays to the **fire commissioner** as **treasurer of the fire department,** a tax of two per cent. on all premiums paid " or agreed to be paid " to him as agent of any insurance company not incorporated under the laws of the State of New York, for insurance upon property in the city during the year ending the first of the preceding September.—*Charter, section* 799.

Every such agent renders to the **fire commissioner** "a just and true account, verified by his oath, of all such premiums."—*Charter, section* 800.

On or before this day the **fire commissioner** may make a written demand upon any such agent, for such account and for the payment of the tax.—*Charter, section* 804.

Terms of three members of the **school board of the borough of Queens,** and of three members of the **school board of the borough of Richmond,** appointed in January, begin.—*Charter, section* 1,061, *paragraph* 3.

On or before this day the trustees of the **College of the City of New York** transmit to the **municipal assembly** and to the secretary of the **board of regents of the University of the State of New York** a **report** for the preceding calendar year.—*Charter, section* 1,133.

On or before this day the trustees of the **Normal College of the City of New York,** transmit to the **municipal assembly** and to the secretary of the **board of regents of the University of the State of New York** a **report** for the preceding calendar year.—*Charter, section* 1144.

On or before this day, the **state comptroller** makes an apportionment of the **school money** assigned to that part of **Queens County** which is included in the City of New York.—*Charter, section* 1,596.

[But see note under October 1st.]

On or before this day "the person appointed to supervise the publication of the **City Record**" certifies "to the **comptroller** that the several lists of officials and employees of departments have been furnished to him" by the **heads of departments.**—*Charter, section* 1,528, *as amended by chap.* 615, *laws* 1900.

[NOTE.—It is probably safe to construe this section as meaning that the person appointed to supervise the publication of the City Record shall certify whether, etc.]

FEBRUARY 11TH.

On or before this day every person acting in the city as agent for a foreign fire insurance company reports his business address to the **fire commissioner.**—*Charter, section* 805.

MARCH 1ST.

After this day the **comptroller,** with the approval of the **board of estimate and apportionment,** may transfer to the **general fund** any unexpended balance of an appropriation or an account, to be "applied "to the reduction of taxation"—. *Charter, section* 237.

[NOTE.—The language of the section is "not less than sixty days after "the expiration of the year for which such appropriations are made".]

"Any remission or reduction of **taxes** upon the real estate of "individuals or corporations must be made within six months after the "delivery of the books to the receiver of taxes for the collection of such "tax".—*Charter, section* 897.

[NOTE.—Under section 911, books are delivered to the receiver on or be- "fore the first day of September".]

MARCH 20TH.

"No vessel, other than **canal boats,** barges or lighters receiving "or delivering property from or to said canal boats or barges, shall use "or enter into for the purpose of using any part of the port of New York "set apart for the use of canal boats and barges, without the written con-

"sent of the **board of docks** had and obtained therefor, and then only "between the first day of January and twentieth day of March in each "year, and when not occupied by canal boats".—*Charter, section* 866.

APRIL 1ST.

On or before this day each board of **inspectors of common schools** makes "a written report to the proper **school board** in respect "to the condition of the schools, the efficiency of teachers, the wants of "the district, especially in regard to schools and school premises".—*Charter, section* 1,098.

From this day to the 31st of October, both inclusive, it is unlawful to kill, capture, or sell any "**bird of song**".—*Charter, section* 1,493.

IN MAY.

The **commissioners of taxes and assessments** act upon applications for reduction of **assessed valuations** of either personal or real property filed in their office before May.—*Charter, section* 895.

MAY 1ST.

The **mayor**, the **comptroller**, and the **chamberlain**, by a majority vote, fix the rate of **interest** to be paid by banks and trust companies upon the city's daily balances during the ensuing three months.—*Charter, section* 196.

From the second Monday in January until this day, the books entitled "The Annual Record of the Assessed Values of Real and Per-"sonal Estate of the Borough of ——— " are kept open for "examination and correction", in the several offices established by the **department of taxes and assessments**.—*Charter, section* 892.

At any time before this day, the **tax commissioners** may transfer from the tax rolls of one borough to those of the proper borough, the name of any person who is improperly assessed for personal taxes in the first borough.—*Charter, section* 894, *as amended by chap.* 500, *laws* 1899.

At any time before this date the **board of taxes and assessments** may increase "the **assessed valuation** of any real or personal estate" of any individual or corporation, as in its judgment may be necessary for the equalization of taxation.—*Charter, section* 896.

At any time before the closing of the books of annual record on this day the **board of taxes and assessments** may decrease the **assessed valuation** of real property.—*Charter, section* 896.

Between the first Monday in January and this day, the **deputy tax commissioners** designated for the purpose in each borough, "receive applications for the revision and cancellation of any assessments "entered in the books of annual record of the **assessed valuation** of "real and personal estate in that borough", "take testimony on such applications", and make recommendations to the department as to the applications.—*Charter, section* 898.

The **board of taxes and assessments** begins the preparation of **assessment rolls** for each borough.—*Charter, section* 907.

All **licenses** issued by the **police department** for public exhibitions expire on this day.—*Charter, section* 1,473.

MAY 5TH.

After the annual record of **assessed valuation** of real and personal estate is opened for correction and review, on the second Monday of January, the **board of taxes and assessments** may not increase the valuation of any property, "except upon notice given to the individual "or corporation affected by such increase at least ten days before the "fifteenth day of May in each year".—*Charter, section* 896.

MAY 20TH.

Any person notified by the tax commissioners that the assessment of his personal property, for purposes of taxation, has been transferred from the tax rolls of one borough to the tax rolls of another borough, "may apply for correction of such assessment on or before the twentieth "day of May, with the same force and effect as if such application were "made on or before the thirtieth day of April, in any year."—*Charter, section* 894, *as amended by chap.* 500, *laws* 1899.

JUNE 1ST.

On or before this day, every **railroad company** operating or using "steam or horse-cars," "in those portions of the city heretofore known "as the City of Brooklyn", certifies "to the **city clerk** the average "number of cars daily operated and used by said company."—*Charter, section* 49.

On or before this day the **mayor** appoints a member of the board of trustees of the **College of the City of New York**, to serve for a term of nine years from the 1st of July.—*Charter, section* 1,128, *as amended by chap.* 757, *laws* 1900.

The **comptroller** pays "to the treasurers of the several volunteer fire companies" in the Borough of Richmond the amounts prescribed. —*Charter, section* 722, *as amended by chap.* 612, *laws* 1899.

The **receiver of taxes** makes a return to the **collector of assessments and arrears**, of all **taxes** and **water rates** remaining unpaid. —*Charter, section* 1,023.

IN JULY.

"Each **school board** shall transmit to the **board of education** an "estimate in detail of the moneys needed within the territory under its jurisdiction during the next succeeding calendar year."—*Charter, section* 1,064, *as amended by chap.* 751, *laws* 1900.

"There shall be published in the **City Record** within the month "of January and within the month of July in each year a **list of all the** "**officials and employees** employed in any of the departments, bureaus "or offices of the city government, and of the counties therein con-"tained, who have been or have become such officials or employees dur-"ing the preceding six months. Said lists shall contain the name, resi-"dence by street numbers, nature of position or service, date of entrance "into the service or employment, date of cessation of such service or "employment, if such has occurred during said period, salary or wages, "and a distinct statement of the increase or decrease thereof during said "period of each of said officials or employees''.—*Charter, section* 1,528, *as amended by Chapter* 615, *laws of* 1900.

FIRST MONDAY IN JULY.

The **assessment rolls** are delivered by the **board of taxes and assessments** to the **municipal assembly.**—*Charter, section* 907.

The **municipal assembly** meets at noon, for the purpose of receiving the **assessment rolls** from the **board of taxes and assessments,** and "of performing such other duties in relation thereto as are "prescribed by law''.—*Charter, section* 907.

JULY 1ST.

On or before this day every **railroad company** operating or using "steam or horse cars," "in that portion of the city heretofore known "as the City of Brooklyn," pays to the **chamberlain** the license fee established by the municipal assembly for the "average number of cars "daily operated and used by said company."—*Charter, section* 49.

On or before this day each **board of inspectors of common schools** makes its quarterly "written **report** to the proper **school board** in re- "spect to the condition of the schools, the efficiency of teachers, and "wants of the district, especially in regard to schools and school premi- "ses."—*Charter, section* 1,098.

The term of office of a member of the board of trustees of the **College of the City of New York,** appointed by the mayor for a term of nine years, begins.—*Charter, section* 1,128, *as amended by chap.* 757, *laws* 1900.

JULY 31ST.

The **state school year** ends.—*Charter, section* 1,084.

AUGUST 1st.

The **mayor,** the **comptroller,** and the **chamberlain,** by a majority vote, fix the rate of **interest** to be paid by banks and trust companies upon the city's daily balances during the ensuing three months.—*Charter, section* 196.

Unpaid **water rents** become "subject to an additional charge of five per cent."—*Charter, section* 476.

Between this day and the 30th day of September the **board of education** transmits "to the **state superintendent of public instruc-" tion** a **report** in writing for the state school year ending on the next "preceding 31st of July, which report shall be in such form and shall "state such facts as the state superintendent and the school law of "the state shall require."—*Charter, section* 1,084.

Between this day and the 30th of November, the **board of education** transmits "to the **mayor** a **report** in writing, bearing date on "the thirty-first day of July next preceding, stating," the particulars called for by the charter.—*Charter, section* 1,085.

On or before this day the "person appointed to supervise the publication of the **City Record** " certifies "to the **Comptroller** that the several lists" of officials and employees of departments "have been furnished to him" by the **heads of departments.**—*Charter, section* 1528, *as amended by chap.* 615, *laws* 1900.

IN SEPTEMBER.

"Two months before the election of municipal officers," in every odd-numbered year, the **comptroller** publishes in the **City Record** and the **corporation newspapers** a detailed statement of the city's receipts and expenditures.—*Charter, section* 161.

FIRST TUESDAY IN SEPTEMBER.

Deputy tax commissioners "commence to assess real and "personal estate."—*Charter, section* 889.

SEPTEMBER 1ST.

The yearly amount due on **assessment** for the "construction of lateral sewers for private owners" becomes "a lien upon the lands or parcels of land affected thereby."—*Charter, section* 567 (*sec. added by chap.* 568, *laws* 1899).

On or before this day each **commissioner of parks** prepares and presents to the **park board** "an itemized estimate of his necessary "expenses for the ensuing fiscal year."—*Charter, section* 617.

On or before this day each **commissioner of buildings** prepares "an itemized estimate of his net expenses for the ensuing fiscal year," and presents it to the **board of buildings.**—*Charter, section* 651.

"On or before" this day each **commissioner of public charities** of the City of New York presents to the **board of public charities** "an "itemized estimate of his necessary expenses for the ensuing fiscal "year."—*Charter, section* 674.

On or before this day, the **commissioner of correction** prepares for presentation to the **board of estimate and apportionment** "an "itemized estimate of the necessary expenses of his department for the "ensuing fiscal year."—*Charter, section* 703.

On or before this day the **municipal assembly** delivers to the **receiver of taxes** the **assessment rolls** for each borough, in final form, with appropriate warrants requiring him to proceed to collect the **taxes.** —*Charter, section* 911.

Immediately after receiving from the municipal assembly the assessment rolls upon a day before this date, the **receiver of taxes** advertises that "the **assessment rolls** have been delivered to him, and that all "taxes are then due and payable at his office in the said respective "boroughs."—*Charter, section* 914.

On or before this day the trustees of the **College of the City of New York** report to the **board of estimate and apportionment** the sum needed for the use of the college, not exceeding $175,000.—*Charter, section* 1,131.

SEPTEMBER 30TH.

Between the first of August and this day, the **board of education** transmits "to the **state superintendent of public instruction** a "**report** in writing for the state school year ending on the next pre-" ceding thirty-first day of July, which report shall be in such form and " shall state such facts as the state superintendent and the school laws " of the state shall require".—*Charter, section* 1,084.

IN OCTOBER.

" Within one hundred and eight hours after the close of each annual registration", the lists of registered **voters** are published in the **City Record.**—*Charter, section* 1,527.

SECOND MONDAY IN OCTOBER.

The **inspectors of common schools** " appointed for the respective " districts in any borough shall organize" — "by the election of one " of their members as chairman and secretary respectively".—*Charter, section* 1,097.

OCTOBER 1ST.

The **board of estimate and apportionment** "shall annually, " between the first day of October and the first day of November, meet, " and by the affirmative vote of all the members make a **budget** of the " amounts estimated to be required to pay the expenses of conducting " the public business of the City of New York, as constituted by this " act, for the then next ensuing year".—*Charter, section* 226.

The **mayor** appoints **inspectors of common schools** in place of those whose terms expire on this day.—*Charter, section* 1,097.

On or before this day each **board of inspectors of common schools** makes its quarterly " written **report** to the proper **school** " **board** in respect to the condition of the schools, the efficiency of " teachers, and wants of the district, especially in regard to schools and " school premises".—*Charter, section* 1,098.

The **state comptroller** shall have power and is hereby authorized "to determine on or before the first day of October in each year the "amount of the county charges and expenses which should be equitably "borne by that part of the **County of Queens** situated within the City "of New York, as hereby constituted, and to **report** the amount thereof "to the **comptroller** of said city".—*Charter, section* 1,593.

On or before this day the **state comptroller** computes and apportions "the amount of the tax for state purposes which should be paid by "that part of the **County of Queens** which is included in the City of "New York, and transmits a statement of the amount to the **comptroller** of the City of New York".—*Charter, section* 1,594.

[NOTE.—By chapter 588 of the laws of 1898, all that part of Queens County not within New York City was made a new county entitled the County of Nassau. The above provisions of secs. 1,593 and 1,594 are, therefore, no longer applicable. It seems to be a necessary presumption that sec. 1,595, cited under "Annually," applies to Queens County. Sec. 1,596 cited under "February 1st," no longer applies, and presumably sec. 1,597 must now apply to Queens County.]

OCTOBER 15TH.

On or before this day the trustees of the **Normal College of the City of New York** report to the **board of estimate and apportionment** a sum not exceeding $150,000 needed for the expenses of the college.—*Charter, section* 1,142.

"No person shall kill or expose for sale, or have in his possession "after the same has been killed, any robin, meadow lark or starling, "between the first day of January and the fifteenth day of October".—Certain cases are excepted.—*Charter, section* 1,493.

OCTOBER 31ST.

It is unlawful to kill, capture, or sell any "**bird of song**" between April 1st and this day, both inclusive.—*Charter, section* 1,493.

FIRST TUESDAY AFTER THE FIRST MONDAY IN NOVEMBER.

Is **election day**.—*Election law, section* 2.

In every second year, beginning with 1897, **aldermen** are elected. —*Charter, section* 24.

In every fourth year, beginning with 1897, the following **officers** are elected:—

The **mayor.**—*Charter, section* 94.

The **comptroller.**—*Charter, section* 97.

Members of the Council.—*Charter, section* 19.

The **president of the council.**—*Charter, section* 18.

A **president of each borough.**—*Charter, section* 382.

Four **coroners** in the Borough of Manhattan, two in the Borough of the Bronx, two in the Borough of Brooklyn, three in the Borough of Queens, and two in the Borough of Richmond.—*Charter, section* 1,570.

NOVEMBER 1ST.

The **mayor,** the **comptroller** and the **chamberlain,** by a majority vote, fix the rate of **interest** to be paid by banks and trust companies upon the city's daily balances during the ensuing three months.—*Charter, section* 196.

The **board of estimate and apportionment** "shall annually, "between the first day of October, and the first day of November, meet, "and by the affirmative vote of all the members make a **budget** of the "amounts estimated to be required to pay the expenses of conducting the "public business of the City of New York, as constituted by this act, for "the then next ensuing year."—*Charter, section* 226.

"**Water taxes** not paid before the first day of November in each "year shall be subject to a further additional charge of ten per cent." This is additional to the five per cent. added on the first of August.—*Charter, section* 476.

Taxes paid on or before this day in the year in which they are levied are reduced by "interest at the rate of six per cent. per annum, between "the day of such payment and the first day of December then next "succeeding."—*Charter, section* 915.

NOVEMBER 30TH.

The year as to which the **commissioners of accounts** report to the

mayor and the **municipal assembly** in the following January, ends on this day."—*Charter, section* 195.

The accounts of the **chamberlain** are closed.—*Charter section* 195.

Between the first day of August and this day the **board of education** transmits to the **mayor** a **report** in "writing bearing date on the "thirty-first day of July next preceding, stating" the particulars called for by the charter.—*Charter, section* 1,085.

IN DECEMBER.

The **commissioners of accounts** examine the accounts of the **chamberlain.**—*Charter, section* 195.

"The **board of estimate and apportionment** shall file with the "final estimate during the month of December in each year a schedule "of the names of all persons not within a department employed under "the city government; the designation of their office and employment, "respectively, and the salaries and compensation fixed for each, which "said schedule shall be published in the **City Record.**"—*Charter, section* 234.

The **general school fund** "shall be apportioned for the next "succeeding calendar year by the **board of education** among the "different **school boards** of the city" in the way laid down by the charter.—*Charter, section* 1065, *as amended by chap.* 751, *laws* 1900.

DECEMBER 1ST.

Annual instalments of **assessments** for the "construction of lateral sewers for private owners" become "due and payable."—*Charter, section* 567 (*sec. added by chap.* 568, *laws* 1899).

The **receiver of taxes** adds one per cent. to the **taxes** for the year not paid by this day.—*Charter, section* 916.

Immediately after this day, the **receiver of taxes** gives "public "notice in the **City Record,** and the corporation newspapers, and in

" such daily paper having a general circulation in any borough as the " **board of city record** may designate, at least ten days, notifying all " persons or corporations who have omitted to pay their taxes, to pay " the same to him at his office in the borough of Manhattan, or to his " several deputies in the several boroughs."—*Charter, section* 919.

DECEMBER 31st.

The **corporation counsel reports** "to the **commissioners of** " **taxes and assessments**" all cases brought by the corporation counsel for the collection of **taxes** on personal property which have been "dis- " missed on account of the inability of the person to pay the tax."—*Charter, section* 934.

DAILY.

The **commissioner of bridges** makes a " daily **report** " to the **comptroller** " of all moneys received or collected by his department " for fares, tolls and any other purposes," and pays the amount to the **chamberlain.**—*Charter, section* 596.

"At the expiration of the office hours for each day and before three "o'clock thereof," the **receiver of taxes** renders to the **chamberlain** a statement of the sums received by the receiver during the day in payment of **taxes.** At the same time the receiver pays over the amount to the chamberlain. Upon the same day, the receiver of taxes exhibits to the **comptroller** the chamberlain's voucher for the amount. In other boroughs than the Borough of Manhattan, **deputies of the receiver of taxes and of the chamberlain** may act in paying over the money collected for taxes during the day.—*Charter, section* 922.

"At the expiration of office hours and on the same day," **the receiver of taxes**, and each deputy receiver to whom taxes are paid, furnishes to the **comptroller** a detailed statement of taxes paid to him during the day.—*Charter, section* 923.

"The **comptroller** shall, on each day, immediately after receiving " from said receiver or deputy the statement, compare the same with the "voucher furnished to him by the chamberlain for the payment there-"of to the chamberlain, and if the aggregate amounts thereof shall cor-"respond, shall credit the said **receiver of taxes** in his books with such "amount."—*Charter, section* 923.

"DAILY (SUNDAYS AND LEGAL HOLIDAYS EXCEPTED.)"

The **City Record** is published.—*Charter, section* 1,526.

WEEKLY.

The **comptroller** furnishes to each **head of department** "weekly a statement of unexpended balances of the appropriation for his department."—*Charter, section* 149.

Each depository of city money makes a weekly statement to the **comptroller.**—*Charter, section* 195.

"Once in each week" the **chamberlain reports** in writing to the **mayor** and the **comptroller** "the moneys received by him, the amount of "all warrants paid by him since his last report, and the amount re-"maining to the credit of the city."—*Charter, section* 196.

The **board of public improvements** meets "once a week at least."—*Charter, section* 412.

"The illuminating **gas** of every company shall be inspected at "least twice a year, and may be inspected as frequently as the **commis-"sioner" (of public buildings, lighting and supplies)** "may think "best, but not oftener than once a week."—*Charter, section* 578.

Each chief officer of an institution in the **department of public charities reports** "once in each week" to the commissioner having charge of the institution, the particulars as to the institution, enumerated in section 680 of the charter.—*Charter, section* 680.

The **sanitary superintendent** and the **assistant sanitary superintendents** "make **reports** weekly or oftener, if required by the

board of health," giving the particulars required by the charter.—*Charter, section* 1,183.

"Once in each week" each **sanitary inspector** makes a written **report** to the **department of health,** giving the particulars required by the charter.—*Charter, section* 1,185.

"Once a week a brief abstract, omitting formal language" ——— "of all transactions" in each **department** of the city government is made, and a copy of it is transmitted "to the person designated to "prepare the **City Record.**"—*Charter, section* 1,546.

All **fees,** perquisites, commissions or percentages received by any municipal **officer** or **department** are paid "weekly" to the **chamberlain.**—*Charter, section* 1,550.

MONTHLY.

"At least one stated meeting" of the **municipal assembly** "shall be held each month, except, in the discretion of the municipal "assembly in August and September."—*Charter, section* 37.

"All **fees** collected by the **city clerk** under and by virtue of" the charter "shall be accounted for and paid over monthly into the treasury "of the city."—*Charter, section* 58.

The **municipal statistical commission** meets "at least once in "each month."—*Charter, section* 132.

On the first Tuesday of the month the **chamberlain** exhibits his bank book to the **comptroller,** "and oftener when required."—*Charter, section* 195.

The **corporation counsel** assigned to the bureau for the recovery of penalties pays "monthly" into the city treasury "all costs and com- "missions received by him from any source whatever," accompanying "the payment with a sworn statement in such form as the comptroller "shall prescribe."—*Charter, section* 259.

"The **treasurer of the police board**, if required by the **comp-**

" **troller,** shall transmit to the **department of finance** each month du- " plicate vouchers for the payment of all sums of money paid on account " of the **police department** during the month."—*Charter, section* 297.

" The said **commissioner of water supply** shall, in every calen- " dar month, file in the office of the **comptroller** of the City of New " York an account of all expenditures made by him, or under his author- " ity, and of all liabilities incurred by him, during the preceding month, " and an abstract of each such account shall be published in the **City** " **Record.**"—*Charter, section* 513.

Each **commissioner of parks** "shall prepare itemized monthly " statements of all receipts and expenditures in duplicate, one of which " statements, together with all vouchers, shall be filed with the " **comptroller,** and one of which shall be filed in his own office."—*Charter, section* 617.

Each **commissioner of buildings** prepares and files similar statements.—*Charter, section* 651.

Each **commissioner of public charities** prepares and files similar statements.—*Charter, section* 674.

The **commissioner of correction** prepares and files similar statements.—*Charter, section* 703.

" Once every month " the **commissioners of public charities** for the boroughs of Manhattan and the Bronx and the commissioners of charities for the boroughs of Brooklyn and Queens collect and pay to the **chamberlain fees** charged to patients not resident in the city treated in the public hospitals.—*Charter, section* 678.

The **receiver of taxes** sends to the **corporation counsel** "monthly" certain cases of personal taxes, described in section 932 of the charter.—*Charter, section* 932.

The **corporation counsel** "or any **marshal** shall pay over, under " oath, to the **receiver of taxes** of said city, monthly, or oftener, if " required, all taxes collected by him."—*Charter, section* 935.

" The **auditor of the board of education** shall transmit to the " **department of finance** each month duplicate vouchers for the payment "of all sums of money made on account of the department of education "each month."—*Charter, section* 1,060, *as amended by chap.* 751, *laws* 1900.

"The **secretary of the board of education** shall certify monthly to "the **comptroller** the amounts" "deducted from the salaries of teachers "during the preceding month," for the **school teachers' retirement fund.**—*Charter, section* 1,083.

Every **justice** before whom any trials for violation of the **sanitary code** or of the rules of the **department of health, reports** "monthly" to the department all such trials and the fines imposed.—*Charter, section* 1,265.

The **department of health** pays to the **police department** "monthly" the amount of the pay of the officers and men of the police detailed as the **sanitary company of the police.**—*Charter, section* 1,324.

QUARTERLY.

[NOTE.—Under this heading are included (1) provision establishing intervals of three months beginning with the first of January, (2) provisions establishing intervals of three months beginning at some other time, and (3) provisions that certain things shall be done "once every three months," "once in three months," etc. The precise meaning of the provisions being doubtful in many cases, it has not been thought safe to go beyond the language of the charter. To a certain extent the same uncertainty affects the entries under "Weekly," "Monthly" and "Semi-Annually."]

"Every three months" the **mayor** renders to the **municipal assembly** "an account of the expenses and receipts of his office," with a statement of the general nature of the duties of his clerks and subordinates, "which account and **report** shall be published in the **City Record.**" —*Charter, section* 117.

"Once in three months" the **commissioners of accounts** "make an examination of the receipts and disbursements in the offices "of the **comptroller** and **chamberlain,** in connection with those of all "the departments and officers making returns thereto, and **report** to the "**mayor** a detailed and classified statement of the financial condition of "the city as shown by such examination."—*Charter, section* 119.

Interest on **stock** and **bonds** of the city is payable quarterly, or semi-annually.—*Charter, section* 169.

"Quarterly, on the first days of February, May, August and No-"vember in each year," the **mayor**, the **comptroller** and the **chamberlain** by a majority vote, fix the rate of **interest** to be paid by banks and trust companies on the city's daily bank balances.—*Charter, section* 196.

The **police board** renders to the **comptroller** "quarterly accounts" of all moneys received by the board for "licenses to runners."—*Charter, section* 349.

Every "charitable and eleemosynary, or reformatory institution "wholly or partly under private control" to which children are committed under provisions of the charter, files with the **commissioner of public charities** for the borough in which the institution is situated, a "list of all such children received, discharged or otherwise disposed of "in the interval."—*Charter, section* 667.

[NOTE.—This section requires that the first list shall be filed "on or before July first, eighteen hundred and ninety-eight," and other lists "every three months thereafter."]

Until the 17th of January, 1917, the **treasurer of the fire department** renders "quarterly in each year" statements of the amounts collected by him on account of the tax upon **foreign fire insurance companies**, to "the treasurer of the **Exempt Firemen's Benevolent Fund of the City of New York**," to "the treasurer of "the **Firemen's Association of the State of New York**," and to "**the Exempt Firemen's Benevolent Fund Association of the Twenty-third and Twenty-fourth wards of the City of New York** (late town of Morrisania in the county of Westchester), in the county of New York." At the same time, he pays the corresponding amounts to these three corporations.—*Charter, section* 808.

Until the 17th of January, 1917 "the **Exempt Firemen's Benev-**

" **olent Fund Association of the Twenty-third Ward of the City** " **of New York** (late town of Morrisania, in the county of West- " chester)," renders to the **fire commissioner** and to the treasurer " of the **Firemen's Association of the State of New York,** " quarterly " in each year," a " sworn statement in detail of the amounts collected " and received." At the same time, the association pays " to said fire " commissioner, as treasurer, forty-five per centum of the amount so col- " lected and received in each quarter, for the use and benefit of the **re- " lief fund of the fire department** of the City of New York, and to " the treasurer of the Firemen's Association of the State New York, ten " per centum of the amount so collected and received."—*Charter, section* 808.

The trustees of the **Exempt Firemen's Benevolent Fund of the City of New York** renders quarterly to the **fire commissioner,** and to the treasurer of the **Firemen's Association of the City of New York,** a sworn detailed statement of the amount received by the trustees. At the same time, they pay over the amounts collected by them, in the manner prescribed by the charter.—*Charter, section* 808.

" Quarterly in each year " the **fire commissioner** renders to each of the associations named in section 809 of the charter " a sworn state- " ment in detail of the amounts collected and received by him " on account of the **tax upon foreign fire insurance companies** doing business in the borough of Brooklyn.—*Charter, section* 809.

" Quarterly in each year" the **Fire Commissioner** makes "to the treasurers of the exempt or veteran volunteer firemen's associations existing in the Borough of Richmond" or in the Borough of Queens "at the time this act takes effect" a sworn statement " in detail of the amounts collected and received by him" on account of the **tax upon foreign fire insurance companies** doing business in those boroughs respectively. —*Charter, sections* 810, *as amended by chap.* 602, *laws* 1898, and 811 (*added by chap.* 602 *laws* 1898).

" At least once in every quarter" the **inspectors of common schools** " visit and inspect all the schools in the district in respect to" the matters enumerated in the charter.—*Charter, section* 1,098.

Each **board of inspectors of common schools** makes a quarterly "written report to the proper **school board** in respect to the condition "of the schools, the efficiency of teachers, and wants of the district, "especially in regard to schools and school premises."—*Charter, section* 1,098.

The **board of pharmacy** meets "at least once every three months." —*Charter, section* 1,513.

"Every three months" the "person appointed to supervise the "publication of the **City Record**" may require the **heads of departments** to furnish information as to the names, salaries, and residences of the subordinates in the departments.—*Charter, section* 1,528.

The executive **departments** of the city government "and all com-"missioners appointed by the mayor, pursuant to the provisions of this "act, and not constituting heads of departments, shall once in three "months and at such other times as the **mayor** may direct, make to him "in such form and under such rules as he may prescribe, **reports** of the "operations and action of the same and each of them, which reports shall "be published in the **City Record.**"—*Charter, section* 1,544.

SEMI-ANNUALLY.

The interest on **city stock and bonds** is payable quarterly or semi-annually.—*Charter, section* 169.

"Illuminating **gas** of every company shall be inspected at least "twice a year, and may be inspected as frequently as the commissioner" (of public buildings, light and supplies) "may think best; but not oftener than once a week."—*Charter, section* 578.

"At the expiration of every six months, it shall be the duty of "said **board of docks** to advertise for one week in the **City Record** and "the **Corporation newspapers** the merchandise, lumber, trucks, wagons "or other obstruction which they have stored and which has remained "unclaimed."—*Charter, section* 853.

The **department of health** makes "semi-annual **reports**" upon the statistics of **tenement houses and lodging houses** to the **state board of health.**"—*Charter, section* 1,175.

"It shall be the duty of the **board ot health** to cause a careful in- "spection to be made of each **tenement and lodging house** at least twice "in each year."—*Charter, section* 1,314.

ANNUALLY.

The "security for the performance of their duties of **trust**" given by any **officers** of the city for security from whom the charter does not make express provision "shall be annually renewed."—*Charter, section* 55.

"At least once in each year," the **mayor,** communicates "to the "**municipal assembly** a general statement of the finances, government "and improvements of the city."—*Charter, section* 115.

"The **bureau of municipal statistics** shall publish annually, "with the approval of the **board estimate and apportionment,** a "volume to be known as the 'Municipal Statistics of the City of New "York for the year——.'"—*Charter, section* 137.

The **corporation counsel** furnishes "to the **board of estimate** "**and apportionment** in each year, at the time of making the estimates "for the ensuing year," a list of the reports of the commissioners of estimate and assessment confirmed for the twelve preceding months with a statement of the amount of awards and costs taxed in each proceeding.—*Charter, section* 175.

"Each year, at the time of making the estimate for the ensuing "year," the **comptroller** furnishes to the **board of estimate and apportionment** a statement of the condition of the **fund for street and park openings,** giving the particulars required by the charter. The **municipal assembly** and the board of estimate and apportionment include in the annual budget an amount sufficient to pay all charges against the fund then outstanding.—*Charter, section* 175.

The **municipal assembly** and the **board of estimate and apportionment** insert in the **annual budget** "an amount to be "estimated by the **comptroller**" to be paid into the **sinking fund of the City of New York.**—*Charter, section* 206.

"At least thirty days before the said" (annual) "**budget** is hereby "required to be made," all **heads of departments** and others required to make **departmental estimates,** submit them to the **board of estimate and apportionment.**—*Charter, section* 226.

[NOTE.—This section requires that the board of estimate shall make the budget "between the first day of October and the first day of November".]

The first meeting of the **board of estimate and apportionment** in every year is "called by notice from the **mayor.**"—*Charter, section* 226.

Within ten days after the members of the **board of estimate and apportionment** have signed the final **budget,** the board presents the budget to the **municipal assembly,** "whereupon a special joint meeting of "the two houses constituting the municipal assembly shall be called to "consider such budget, and the same shall simultaneously be published in the **City Record.**"—*Charter, section* 226.

The **comptroller** submits to the **municipal assembly** at least four weeks before the annual meeting of the assembly held for the purpose of imposing the annual taxes "a statement setting forth the amounts by law "authorized to be raised by tax" in that year for city purposes, "and "also an estimate of the probable amount of receipts by the city treasury "during the then current year, from all sources of revenue," of the general fund.—*Charter, section* 247. *Same provisions in section* 900.

The **comptroller** certifies to the **municipal assembly** "the "aggregate amount estimated by the municipal assembly and the board "of estimate and apportionment, in the **annual budget.**"—*Charter, section* 249.

"It shall be the duty of said **municipal assembly,** in joint session "of both houses, and they are hereby empowered and directed annually "to cause to be raised, according to law and collected by tax upon the "estates, real and personal, subject to taxation within the City of New "York, the amount so certified, as aforesaid."—*Charter, section* 249.

"Every owner, agent or lessee of a steam **boiler** in use in the City "of New York," **reports** the boiler to the **police department** in the manner required by the rules established by the board of police. All boilers so reported are then inspected by the members of the **sanitary company of police.**—*Charter, seetion* 342.

The **superintendent of elections** renders "to the **police board** "in each year a statement of the operations and expenses of the "general bureau of elections and the branches thereof, together with "an estimate of the expenses thereof for the ensuing year, and such "recommendations in reference to the election law and the rules and "regulations of the police board relating to the election bureau and as to "elections as to him may seem advisable."—*Charter, section* 365.

The **board of public improvements** makes "an annual report to "the **mayor.**"—*Charter, section* 412.

Each commissioner at the **head of a department** who is a member of the board of public improvements makes "an annual **report** of the "business and transactions of his department to the **mayor.**"—*Charter, section* 457.

The **commissioner of highways** makes "an annual **report** of the "business and transactions of his department to the **mayor.**"—*Charter, section* 524.

"The **president of the board of docks** shall be elected annually by the members thereof."—*Charter, section* 828.

The **board of docks** annually presents a **report** to the **mayor.** —*Charter, section* 829.

"The **commissioner of water supply** shall, annually, at the time "the tax levy in each year is confirmed by the municipal assembly

" cause to be prepared and transmitted to the **collector of assess-" **ments and arrears** a separate account for each **ward** of all lots on " which **water rents** for that year " . . . " may remain unpaid."—*Charter, section* 1,022.

The **board of education** distributes the **general school fund** among the **school boards** in the manner prescribed by the charter.—*Charter, section* 1,065, *as amended by chap.* 751, *laws of* 1900.

The **board of education** appoints annually at least three members of the board to act as " an executive committee for the care, government " and management of" the **nautical school.**—*Charter, section* 1,158.

" After such completion of the assessment rolls or tax books, it shall " be the duty of the **city clerk** to procure the proper warrants author-" izing and requiring the **receiver of taxes** to collect the several sums " therein mentioned." The warrants, properly signed, are then immediately delivered by the **president of the council** to the receiver of taxes, and at the same time the president of the council notifies the **comptroller** of " the amount of **taxes** in each book, in order that he may " cause the proper sum to be charged to the receiver for collection."—*Charter, section* 909.

The **department of health** makes to the **mayor** "an annual " **report** of all the operations of the department for the previous year." —*Charter, section* 1,168.

The **controller of the state** annually transmits to the **comptroller of the City of New York** a statement of the amount of tax for " state " purposes to be paid by the **counties of New York, Kings and** " **Richmond,** respectively."—*Charter, section* 1,595.

[See note under " October 1st ".]

EVERY FIVE YEARS.

" Each **school board** shall have power every five years, if it shall " have once divided the territory into **inspection districts,** again to " divide it into such districts, and to make changes in existing districts, " or their number."—*Charter, section* 1,097.

INDEX TO CALENDAR OF NEW YORK CITY CHARTER.

	SECTION CHARTER.	PAGE CALENDAR.
By fire insurance agents	805	10
Of number of street cars operated	49	13
By street railroad companies	49	13
By board of education	1,084	15, 17
By board of education	1,085	15, 20
By comptroller on Queens County taxes	1,594	18
By receiver of taxes	922	21
By receiver of taxes	923	21
By commissioner of bridges	596	21
By corporation counsel	934	21
By depositories of city's money	195	22
By chamberlain	196	22
By sanitary and assistant sanitary superintendents	1,183	22
By chief officers of institutions in department of charities	680	22
By sanitary inspectors	1,185	23
By assistant corporation counsel assigned to the bureau for the recovery of penalties	259	23
By sanitary inspectors	1,185	23
By commissioner of correction	703	24
By commissioners of public charities	674	24
By commissioners of public buildings	651	24
By commissioners of parks	617	24
By commissioner of water supply	513	24
By mayor	117	25
By justices	1,265	25
By commissioners of accounts	119	25
By treasurer of fire department	808	26
By certain private charitable institutions	667	26
By chief officers of institutions	667	26
By firemen's funds	808	27

www.ingramcontent.com/pod-product-compliance
Lightning Source LLC
LaVergne TN
LVHW020626110826
845149LV00004B/1046
9781418186791